Bilingual Edition
READING POWER
WITHDRAWN
Edición Bilingüe

(Record-Breaking Animals)

The Blue Whale
World's Largest Mammal

La ballena azul:
El mamífero más grande del mundo

Joy Paige

The Rosen Publishing Group's
PowerKids Press™ & **Buenas Letras**™

Published in 2003 by The Rosen Publishing Group, Inc.
29 East 21st Street, New York, NY 10010

First Bilingual Edition 2003
First Edition in English 2002

Book Design: Sam Jordan
Photo Credits: Cover, pp. 7, 12–13, 18–19 © Mike Johnson; pp. 5, 8–9 © Innerspace Visions; p. 9 © Kim Sayer/Corbis; pp. 10–11 © Corbis; pp. 14–15, 17 © Animals Animals; pp. 20–21 © Noaa.gov

Paige, Joy
The Blue Whale: World's largest mammal/La Ballena Azul: El mamífero más grande del mundo/Joy Paige ; traducción al español: Spanish Educational Publishing
p. cm. — (Record-Breaking Animals)
Includes bibliographical references and index.
ISBN 0-8239-6896-0 (lib. bdg.)
1. Blue whale—Juvenile literature. [1. Blue whale. 2. Whales. 3. Spanish Language Materials—Bilingual.] I. Title.

Printed in The United States of America

Contents _____

The Largest Mammal   4

Swimming   14

Food   18

Glossary   22

Resources   23

Index   24

_____ Contenido

El mamífero más grande   4

Grandes nadadoras   15

¿Qué comen?   19

Glosario   22

Recursos   23

Índice   24

The blue whale is the
largest mammal.

La ballena azul es
el mamífero más grande
del mundo.

Blue whales live in oceans all over the world. They are on the endangered species list.

Las ballenas azules viven
en los océanos de todo
el mundo.
Están en peligro de extinción.

Arctic
Ocean
Océano
Ártico

North
Atlantic
Ocean
Océano
Atlántico
Norte

North
Pacific
Ocean
Océano
Pacífico
Norte

North
Pacific
Ocean
Océano
Pacífico
Norte

Indian
Ocean
Océano
Índico

South
Pacific
Ocean
Océano
Pacífico
Sur

South
Atlantic
Ocean
Océano
Atlántico
Sur

Blue whales can grow to be over 100 feet (30m) long. Their hearts are the size of small cars.

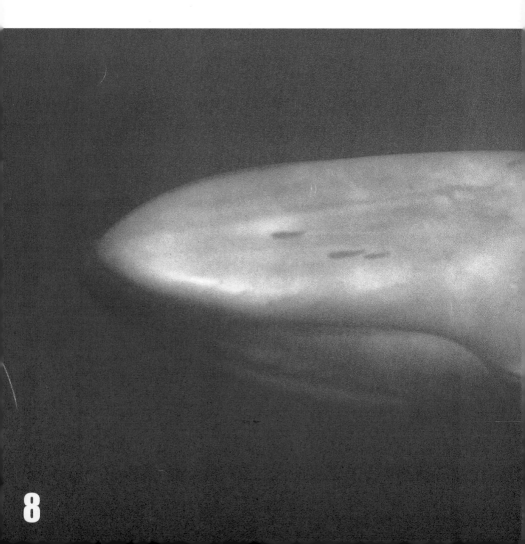

Las ballenas azules pueden
medir 100 pies (30m) de largo.
Su corazón es del tamaño
de un auto pequeño.

Heart =
Corazón =

Blue whales are heavy.
They can weigh between
200,000 and 300,000
pounds (90 to 136t).
That is the weight of
21 elephants!

Las ballenas azules pesan de 200,000 a 300,000 libras (90 a 136t): ¡lo mismo que 21 elefantes!

Blue whale babies are called calves. Calves are about 23 feet (7m) long and weigh about 5,000 pounds (2.2t) when they are born.

Las crías de las ballenas azules se llaman ballenatos. Miden unos 23 pies (7m) de largo y pesan unas 5,000 libras (2.2t) al nacer.

Blue whales have very large tails. Their tails help them swim fast. Blue whales can swim up to 30 miles (48.2km) an hour.

Las ballenas azules tienen
una cola muy grande.
Así nadan muy rápido.
Las ballenas azules pueden
nadar a 30 millas (48.2km)
por hora.

Blue whales breathe from two blowholes on the top of their bodies. Blue whales can hold their breath for an hour!

Las ballenas azules respiran por dos orificios nasales en la parte de arriba del cuerpo. ¡Las ballenas azules pueden contener la respiración durante una hora!

Blowholes
Orificios nasales

Blue whales eat other sea animals. Their favorite food is krill. Sometimes they eat as much as 40 million krill a day!

Las ballenas azules comen
otros animales marinos.
Su alimento preferido es el krill.
¡Comen 40 millones de krill
al día!

The blue whale is the largest mammal that has ever lived!

¡La ballena azul es el mamífero más grande que ha existido en la Tierra!

21

Glossary

blowholes (**bloh**-hohlz) the openings on a whale's head that allow air in

breathe (**breeth**) to take air into the lungs and force it out

calves (**cavz**) baby whales

endangered species (en-**dane**-jurhd **spee**-ceez) a group of animals or plants that might stop living on Earth

krill (**krihl**) a type of sea life that whales eat

mammal (**mam**-uhl) a warm-blooded animal

Glosario

alimento (el) comida

ballenato (el) cría de ballena

krill (el) animal marino que comen las ballenas

mamífero (el) animal de sangre caliente

orificios nasales (los) agujeros de la cabeza por donde respiran las ballenas

peligro de extinción posibilidad de que una especie de planta o animal desaparezca de la Tierra

respirar llenar los pulmones de aire y dejarlo salir

Resources / Recursos

Here are more books to read about the Blue Whale:
Otros libros que puedes leer sobre las ballenas azules:

Blue Whales
by Patricia Miller-Schroeder
Raintree Steck-Vaughn Publishers (1998)

The Blue Whale
by Melissa Kim
Hambleton-Hill Publishing (1993)

Web sites
Due to the changing nature of Internet links, PowerKids Press has developed an online list of Web sites related to the subject of this book. This site is updated regularly. Please use this link to access the list:

Sitios web
Debido a las constantes modificaciones en los sitios de Internet, PowerKids Press ha desarrollado una guía on-line de sitios relacionados al tema de este libro. Nuestro sitio web se actualiza constantemente. Por favor utiliza la siguiente dirección para consultar la lista:

http://www.buenasletraslinks.com/chl/tmb

Word count in English: 157
Número de palabras en español: 173

Index

B
blowholes, 16–17

C
calves, 12

H
heart, 8–9

K
krill, 18

M
mammal, 4, 20

O
ocean, 6–7

T
tails, 14

Índice

B
ballenato, 13

C
cola, 15
corazón, 9

K
krill, 19

M
mamífero, 4, 20

O
océano, 6–7
orificios nasales, 16–17

2/09 ④ 8/08
1/10 ⑤ 1/10
7/12 ⑦ 5/12
8/14 ⑧ 5/13
7/18 ⑭ 7/18